So You Want to Learn About

Butterflies

Written and Photographs by
Katrina Willoughby

© Willoughby Arts 2018

I hear you want to learn about butterflies. These beautiful creatures with wings of many colors flutter in the daylight. They bring joy and wonder to our lives. This book will help you learn more about them!

Butterflies are found across the world. They are on every continent except Antarctica.

You can't be bitten or stung by a butterfly.

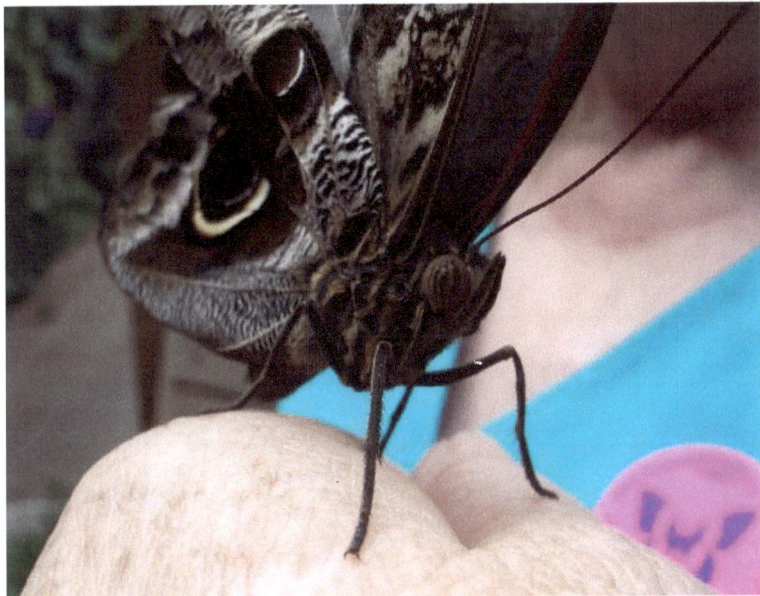

Each butterfly has four wings. There are 2 pairs of wings; the front set are called the forewing and the back set are called the hindwing.

The inside and the outside of the wings may look very different.

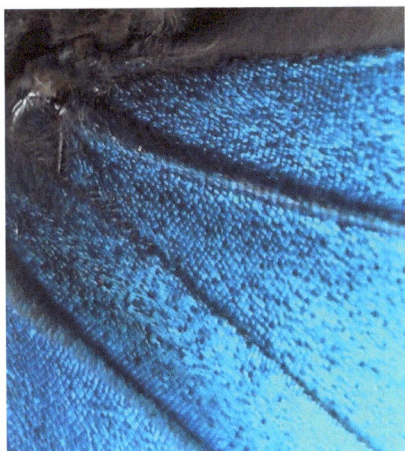

Wings on butterflies are covered with tiny scales. Each scale is a single color.

Butterflies come in many different colors. Some are bright and easy to pick out while others are camouflaged to match the plants around them. Camouflage helps a butterfly hide.

The butterfly above looks just like a leaf!

You may wonder why a butterfly would be bright colors. In the wild, bright colors can be a warning that something is poisonous.

While some butterflies are poisonous if eaten, others trick predators by wearing bright colors and pretending to be poisonous.

Unlike you and me, a butterfly can't control its body temperature. They are cold blooded which means their temperature changes with the world around them. A butterfly needs to be warm enough to fly. When it is cool out you may see butterflies sunning themselves to get warm so they can take flight.

Butterflies don't have eyelids so they can't shut their eyes. They have compound eyes with thousands of tiny lenses. These let them see a wide area and easily detect motion. They can't see very well far away. Butterflies can see ultraviolet light. Humans don't see this.

Most butterflies fly between 5 to 12 miles per hour, but the fastest butterflies can fly up to 37 miles per hour.

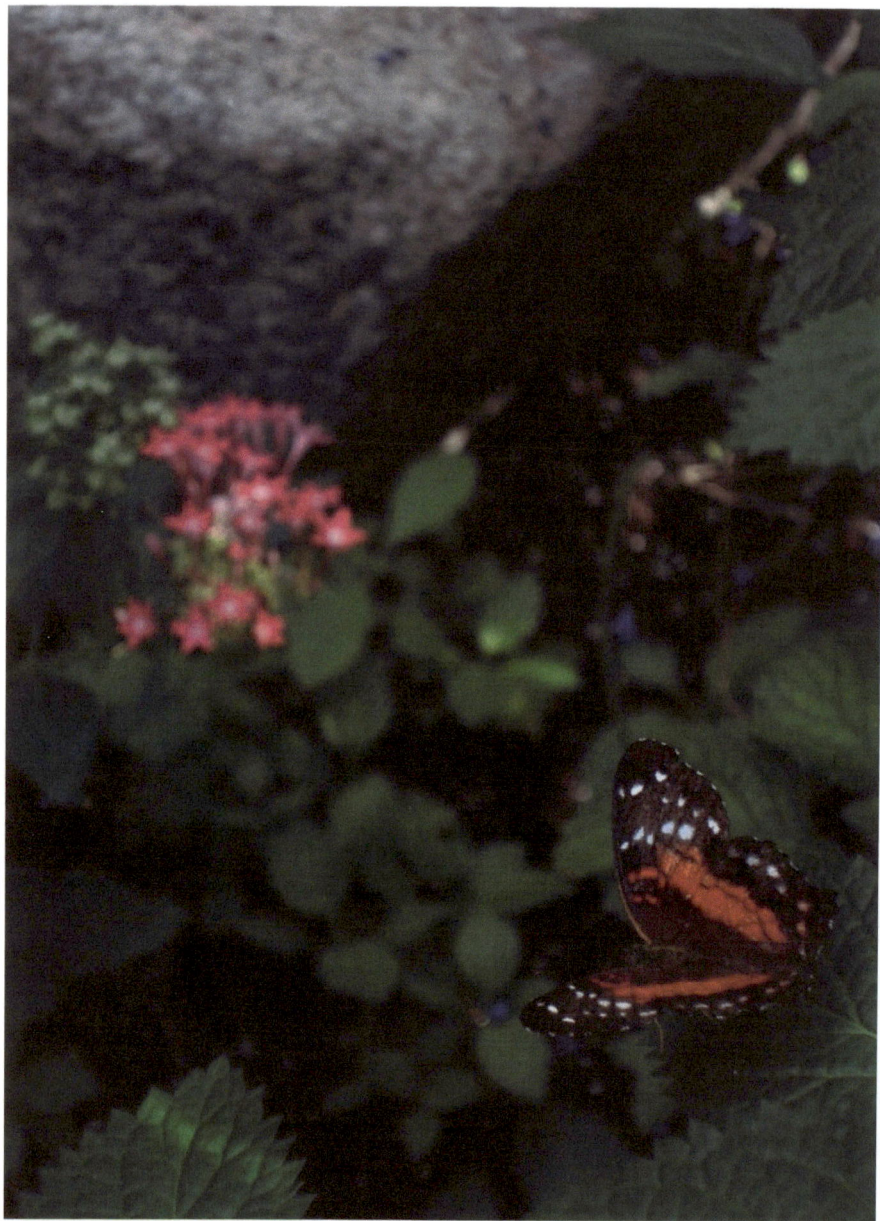

Many animals migrate. This is when a species of animal move from one part of the country or world to another. Some butterflies migrate too. The monarch butterflies travel thousands of miles to go south for the winter. Groups of monarchs can travel all the way from Canada to Mexico! This is the largest insect migration in North America.

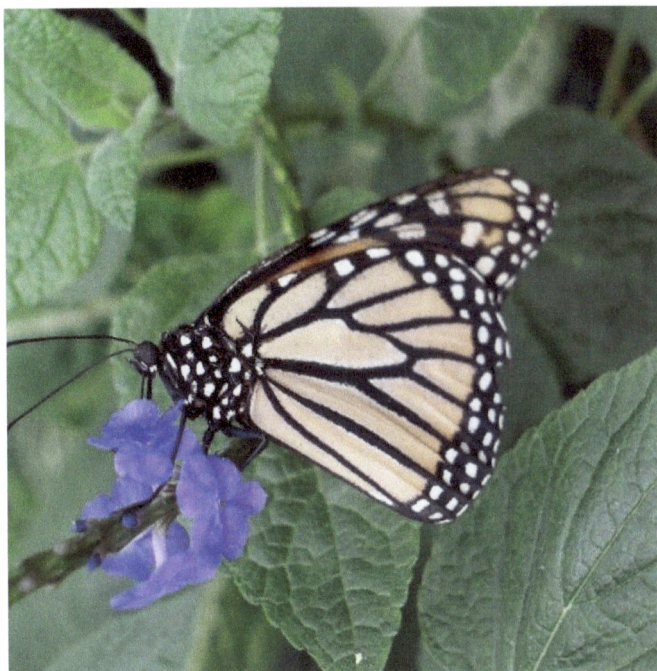

This is a picture of a monarch butterfly.

You can plant a butterfly garden to try and attract butterflies to your yard. The plants that are chosen have to be ones that butterflies and their caterpillars want to eat. To do this right, you will need to research the types of butterflies that live near you and what they eat.

A butterfly will only lay eggs on plants that the caterpillars will eat. Caterpillars are picky eaters. Many will only eat one type of plant. An example of this is the monarch caterpillar. They only eat milkweed.

This picture is a monarch caterpillar with the flowers of a milkweed that grows in Texas.

There are 4 stages to the butterfly life cycle

A female butterfly lays little eggs on a leaf. Remember that they will only lay eggs on leaves that the caterpillar will eat. After a caterpillar hatches it eats a lot and grows quickly.

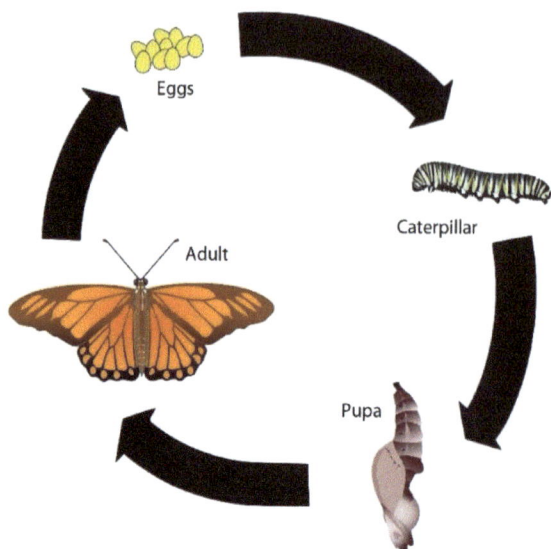

Eggs

Caterpillar

Adult

Pupa

The caterpillar makes a pupa. This is the casing it will stay in while it turns into a butterfly. This is called metamorphosis; when it changes into something different than what it was.

When metamorphosis is done the pupa opens up and a beautiful winged creature emerges.

When it rains butterflies must hide from the rain drops. They will hang under leaves and cling to tree trucks to stay dry and safe.

Wings repel water but if a butterfly gets wet it can't fly until it is dry. Have you ever seen a butterfly walking around waiting to dry after the rain?

Butterflies are a type of insect. Just like other insects they have 6 jointed legs. Each leg has six parts.

Some butterflies can use their feet to determine if the plant they are on is the kind their caterpillars would like to eat.

They have sensors that act like taste buds. If the plant is right, they can lay eggs on it.

Butterflies have a lot of sensors to detect smells.

They have sensors on their heads, antenna, feet and abdomen.

It may appear that some butterflies have a nose. This pointy end on their faces is called the palpi.

It does have sensors on it to pick up different odors, but they don't use it to breathe.

Since a butterfly is an insect, they don't have lungs. Like other insects they have tiny openings called spiracles on their body. Tubes allow air to enter the butterfly's respiratory system.

The black dots on this butterfly's abdomen are the spiracles.

On this caterpillar they are orange.

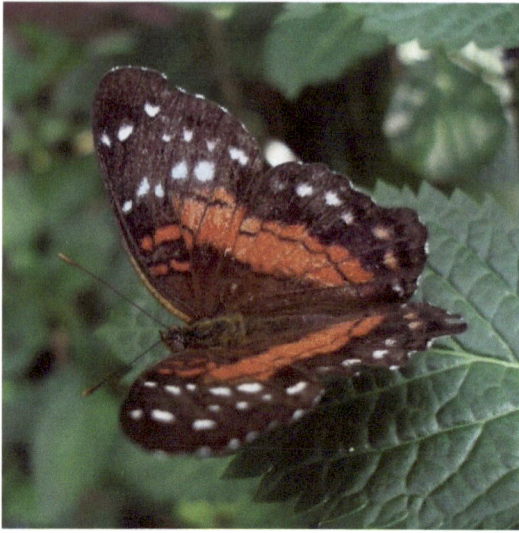

Antennae are used for a sense of smell and balance. The butterfly can control and move their antennae.

Without antennae, a butterfly can't fly where it wants, it may be stuck flying in circles.

A butterfly's tongue is called a proboscis.

Nectar from flowers is sipped up using the proboscis. The proboscis can be held curled up and unwound to use like a straw when it is time to eat.

Small muscles control coiling and uncoiling the butterfly's proboscis.

In captivity flower, fruit and a sugary solution are used to nourish butterflies.

Did you know that a group of butterflies is called a flutter or swarm? Some people call a group of butterflies a kaleidoscope.

A group of caterpillars is known as an army.

Butterfly houses are buildings that ship in butterfly pupas from around the world. They hatch the butterflies and put them on display for the people to enjoy and researchers to study.

You can walk in a room with butterflies all around.

In a butterfly house you have to watch where you step to make sure a butterfly hasn't landed in the path. Sometimes they come land on you!

If you haven't visited a butterfly house I hope you get to one day!

So….

Did you learn new things about butterflies?

I hope you learned new things and enjoyed this book!

This is the first book in the series "So You Want to Learn About…" Please check for other books.

Thank you for reading.

Other books in this series

So You Want to Learn About Turtles & Tortoises

So You Want to Learn About Reptiles & Amphibians

So You Want to Learn About Insects & Bugs

www.ingramcontent.com/pod-product-compliance
Lightning Source LLC
Chambersburg PA
CBHW041224270326
41933CB00001B/36